# Two Besides

Alan Bennett has been a leading dramatist since *Beyond the Fringe* in the 1960s. His works for stage and screen include *Talking Heads*, *Forty Years On*, *The Lady in the Van*, *A Question of Attribution*, *The Madness of George III*, an adaptation of *The Wind in the Willows*, *The History Boys*, *The Habit of Art*, *People*, *Hymn*, *Cocktail Sticks* and *Allelujah!* His collections of prose are *Writing Home*, *Untold Stories* (PEN/Ackerley Prize, 2006) and *Keeping On, Keeping On*. *Six Poets* contains Bennett's selection of English verse, accompanied by his commentary. Recent fiction includes *The Uncommon Reader* and *Smut: Two Unseemly Stories*.

# Alan Bennett

# Two Besides

## A Pair of
## Talking Heads

**ff** P

This edition first published in 2020
by Faber and Faber Limited
74–77 Great Russell Street
London WC1B 3DA
and
Profile Books Ltd
29 Cloth Fair
London EC1A 7JQ
This paperback edition first published in 2021

Typeset by Agnesi Text, Hadleigh, Suffolk
Printed and bound by CPI Group (UK) Ltd, Croydon CR0 4YY

A CIP record for this book is available from the British Library

ISBN 978-0-571-36586-9

2 4 6 8 10 9 7 5 3 1

# Contents

# *Talking Heads* – How They Happened

## NICHOLAS HYTNER

On the evening of Thursday, 26 March 2020, the fourth day of lockdown, I was – like everyone else in my world – strung out somewhere between terror and a loose end. At a loose end because, ten days earlier, the prime minister had (sort of) closed the theatres. (He cleared up the confusion two days later, a crisis-management template that would become familiar.) My own Bridge Theatre went dark. We had got no further than the first day of rehearsals for the show that would have seen us through to the end of June. I was terrified because there was no indication when we'd be able to open again. As I write, there still isn't.

So when my agent, Anthony Jones, called to say that Piers Wenger, the BBC's Head of Drama, wanted me to remake Alan Bennett's *Talking Heads*, I said yes without thinking.

'That is the correct answer,' said my agent.

Then Piers called to tell me what I'd said yes to.

He said that all BBC drama production had halted, that the only films they could imagine making were monologues as anything else would bring actors into close contact with each other. He said that *Talking Heads*, made originally in the 1980s and 1990s, were seminal works that he'd never forgotten, and that they were all studies in isolation, so they'd speak with particular force to the current moment.

Could I imagine, Piers asked, making them with a group of today's leading actors, the equivalents of Eileen Atkins, Thora Hird, Patricia Routledge, Maggie Smith, Julie Walters and Penelope Wilton?

Could I imagine making them while observing all the restrictions imposed by social distancing? Making new content for the BBC was considered essential work – news and current affairs were still up and running – so what about finding a way of shooting drama that keeps everyone, behind the camera as well as in front of it, two metres apart?

Could I imagine making them on pre-existing sets at Elstree Studios, because making new ones would be out of the question, and filming on location was even less viable and, by the way, there are six separate sound stages at Elstree filled with all the interiors they use for *EastEnders*?

And finally: they'd like to have them ready for transmission by June, because in the absence of anything new, the schedules were rapidly filling with repeats. Would that be okay too? Maybe I could start shooting them in three weeks?

I still said yes.

One more thing, said Piers, would I call Alan and persuade him that it was a good idea?

The 'one more thing' started to make sense of the rest. I'm the last person you'd come to in normal times to make seven hours of television. I've never produced or directed television. I've spent my career in the theatre, and I've made a small handful of movies. But since 1990, I've directed all of Alan's new plays and screenplays. He's been the biggest part of my luck. And now, as my colleagues stayed home and became ever more desperate, he became my luck once more. Piers was afraid Alan would say no. Even Anthony Jones, who is Alan's agent as well as mine, was afraid he'd say no. They thought I could persuade him. I said yes, I'd call him, and yes, he'd say yes.

*

I should have felt sick. It takes months, sometimes years, to steer a film, however short and simple, through to the first day of production. I'd just agreed to make twelve short films, all around thirty or forty minutes long, but for the first time in weeks the sickness in the pit of my stomach lifted. The only solution I've ever found to life is work. Without it I'm lost, which has been a curse as well as a blessing. Piers had put the full resources of the BBC at my disposal if I could make *Talking Heads* happen. I figured I had the weekend to come up with a plan, and I was for a brief moment elated.

The first call I made was to Kevin Loader, who has produced two movies with me: *The History Boys* and *The Lady in the Van*, both written by Alan. Both started on stage, and both made a seamless transition to film thanks in large part to Kevin. He's all the things you want in a producer: calm, expert, enthusiastic. He started his career at the BBC and knew it backwards, which didn't hurt either. He didn't miss a beat. He'd call his regular co-producer Steve Clark Hall. I'd call my colleague Nick Starr, with whom I built and now ran the Bridge Theatre. The key to making things happen (and to getting the credit for it) is knowing other people who know more than you do.

The same evening, I spoke to Naomi Donne, the hair and make-up designer who had just been Oscar-nominated for

4

the film *1917*, and was working on the new Batman movie when everyone was sent home. She can do blood-spattered armies, she can do superheroes, and I reckoned if she knew how to do hair and make-up from a two-metre distance, then it might be feasible to imagine the same for everything else – sets, costumes, photography. She asked why it wouldn't be possible for all twelve actors to do their own make-up and hair, under her supervision. She could hold tutorials for them on FaceTime, so that when they came to the set, they'd be ready to deal with themselves, and she could direct them from the other side of the make-up room.

On Friday, Kevin, Nick and I met on Zoom, which became as indispensable as it is depressing. I might learn to love it when it's an option rather than a necessity. Now, via our laptops, we put the basics together. It would have been more fun to have done it in a café.

London Theatre Company – which is the company Nick and I formed to build the Bridge Theatre – would make *Talking Heads* for the BBC. Kevin and I would act as producers. Our lawyer, Medwyn Jones, arranged a contract with BBC Studios, a commercial entity independent of the BBC itself, to provide production and post-production services, sets and crew. We'd find twelve actors and six

5

directors, though I thought I might direct three or four of them myself. We'd bring on board a director of photography, a production designer, a costume designer, a hair and make-up designer, a composer and a casting director.

I went next to Robert Sterne, who has cast all my recent productions at the Bridge Theatre and, with Nina Gold, was responsible for *Game of Thrones*, *The Crown* and countless other high-profile British dramas.

'What do you think?' I asked Robert. 'The idea is to start shooting in around three weeks. We can rehearse only on Zoom. The actors will have to drive themselves to the set. They'll have a single day to shoot upwards of thirty minutes, direct to camera, and these monologues are written to be shot in long, uninterrupted takes, so they'll really have to know them, no safety net.'

'They'll bite your arm off,' said Robert. 'Everyone is stuck at home, itching to work. I'll start making lists.'

I sped through my own list of some of the best actors in the English-speaking world.

'They'll bite your arm off,' he said again. 'How do I get hold of the scripts?'

'I have the published edition on my bookshelves. I guess I'll have to scan it and email it to you.'

That Friday evening, at more or less the same time that the prime minister's chief adviser Dominic Cummings set off on his essential four-hour road trip to Durham, I went on my allotted hour's walk on Primrose Hill and called Alan. I was wearing the kind of headphones that pick up more of what's going on in the world outside than of the voice making the call.

'Could you say that again?' said Alan.

I had to shout it several times before he fully grasped what I was saying. By the time I'd finished, everyone on Primrose Hill knew what the plan was. What I didn't say was that one of the reasons they'd come to me was that they'd thought he'd take a lot of persuading, so could he at least put up some show of reluctance? But he was so touched and amazed that anyone remembered *Talking Heads*, never mind wanted to remake them, that he'd told me to go ahead before I'd had a chance to tell him the whole story.

I called Piers Wenger and Anthony Jones to tell them that, thanks to my compelling eloquence and my long working relationship with him, Alan had given us the green light.

'Do you think', asked Piers, 'you might be able to persuade him to write a new *Talking Head*?'

7

I said, no, I can't do that, finally acknowledging the boundaries of the possible. Alan hasn't written under commission for as long as I've known him. *Talking Heads* is the purest distillation of his work. No way can he or will he rustle one up to order.

'That's okay,' said Piers. 'It's good that we can do the twelve we have.'

An hour later, I remembered that Alan had already written a new *Talking Head*. He'd given it to me a couple of years ago, when we were rehearsing his play *Allelujah!* He'd wondered what we could do with it. I said that maybe once we'd done the play, we could take it to the BBC. I'd put it in a file, and I'd forgotten about it. I went upstairs and fished it out. Underneath was another new *Talking Head*, which I'd also forgotten. I read them again. My pulse beat as fast as it always beats when I'm reading Alan's new stuff. The first was called *Phèdre*; the second had no title.

I called Alan again and told him I'd just found two new *Talking Heads*.

'Oh yes,' he said. 'I'd forgotten about them.'

'They're really good,' I said, 'and the BBC want a new one, so shall we offer them these?'

'I'd better take another look at them before you do,' said Alan, 'but I think I gave you the only copies.' Alan still works on a manual typewriter and doesn't have a computer.

I said I'd photocopy them, go past his house on my walk the next day (we live close to one another), and leave them on his doorstep.

'Give me a moment,' said Alan, 'and I'll see if I took copies for myself.'

He called me back a little later. 'I've found them,' he said. 'They're all right. I'll do a little work on them.'

We went into the weekend with fourteen *Talking Heads*, two producers, one director, a co-producer, a hair and make-up designer, and a production company.

★

At 9 a.m. on Saturday morning, Kevin and I met on Zoom with BBC Studios: Deborah Sathe, the acting Head of Drama Series; Jon Sen, the executive producer of *EastEnders*, and Sue Mather, the *EastEnders* line producer. Over the coming weeks, I got to know their faces and their home offices very well. Accustomed to putting out two hours of drama every week, they weren't unnerved by seven hours or so of *Talking Heads*.

Over Saturday and Sunday, we started to put together the rest of the key creators. Kevin introduced me to Zac Nicholson, the director of photography, and Simon Bowles, the production designer. I called costume designer Jacqueline Durran, who won her second Oscar in 2020 for *Little Women* – she's been nominated seven times.

'I don't know how you'd do this,' I said to her. 'I guess you could ask the actors to take you on a tour of their own wardrobes. Beyond that, I'm at a loss. And I think we have to set them in some kind of non-specific recent past. Most of them were written in the eighties and nineties. Maybe one or two of them have to be specifically eighties.'

'The usual suppliers are closed, but eBay's still working,' she said, undaunted. In the event, that's where most of the costumes came from. They are, in their way, as much a tribute to her eye and her flair as the gorgeous crinolines in *Little Women*. We agreed at the outset that every character in the series should be limited to two costumes. By the time we started shooting, many of the actors had persuaded her they'd be happier wearing something different in each scene, as each new scene marks a new day in their character's life. From somewhere or other, she put together around sixty costumes. Just her.

It was to the actors, and who should direct them, that I now turned my attention. We knew that the monologues would have to be rehearsed remotely, and that director and actor would meet in the flesh for the first and only time on the day of the shoot. It felt like a good idea to match actors, where possible, to directors they already knew. And it felt like another good idea to gather together a group of theatre directors who were used to working in forensic detail on complicated texts. All the *Talking Heads* are written to be shot in a small handful of uninterrupted takes. 'The essential thing about the monologues', Alan wrote to me in a note a few days later, 'is that they are just that – one person talking without a lot of movement. Too much movement makes it look as though there is action whereas all the action is in the story being told.' The six directors I approached – Marianne Elliott, Nadia Fall, Sarah Frankcom, Jonathan Kent, Jeremy Herrin and Josie Rourke – worked together to develop a house style based on a series of restrained, slow-moving shots that put all the emphasis on the actor telling the story. (To be honest, it was a style established by the directors of the first series of *Taking Heads* – Stuart Burge, Giles Foster, Tristram Powell and Alan himself.) During one of our long Zoom conferences, Alan called me to catch up on how everything was going. I held my phone up to the computer screen and he talked direct to all of us for the first and only time.

Robert's shortlist of actors included some that were blindingly obvious (Imelda Staunton, Sarah Lancashire), and some that were wonderfully imaginative (Martin Freeman as Graham, the prissy mother's boy played originally by Alan himself). I shared them with the directors and with Alan. He didn't know the younger ones, but he responded with enthusiasm to the ones he knew, and he was delighted with the idea that Martin Freeman might liberate Graham from his own performance: 'He mustn't do it anything like I did it.'

The first actor I approached was Lesley Manville, who is a close friend.

'Could I try something out on you?' I asked, and I took her through the whole story.

Lesley said that, as it happened, she was quite busy: she'd turned the cupboard under the stairs into a home studio and was spending much of her time recording voice-overs. But that didn't dampen her enthusiasm for learning a forty-five-minute *Talking Head* in less than three weeks, so I felt, as a group of directors, we were safe to start approaching all the other actors. In addition to *Bed Among the Lentils*, I thought I should direct the two new ones. Or maybe it would be more candid to say I nabbed the two new ones as I was damned if I was going to let anyone else get their hands on them. I sounded out two actors I'd long admired from afar: Monica Dolan and Sarah Lancashire. For the rest, Imelda Staunton and Kristin Scott Thomas had established working relationships with Jonathan Kent; Maxine Peake had often worked with Sarah Frankcom; Tamsin Greig and Harriet Walter had both worked with Marianne Elliott; Martin Freeman had worked with Jeremy Herrin, and he was enthusiastic about approaching Lucian Msamati. Nadia Fall knew and had briefly worked with Rochenda Sandall, and Josie Rourke felt like a good match with Jodie Comer. No arranger of marriages has ever had an easier time.

The deal we did with them was unusual. The artists and senior crew involved in *Talking Heads* (writer, actors, directors, producers, director of photography, production designer, costume designer, hair and make-up designer, composer, casting director) decided to donate their fees to NHS Charities Together, to support NHS staff, volunteers and patients as they tackled the Covid crisis.

13

Collectively, we diverted more than £1 million to those who needed it more than we did. An additional benefit was that nobody's agent got to argue about the size of their client's trailer.

Meanwhile, fourteen *Talking Heads* had become twelve again. As Robert and I talked about who might do *A Cream Cracker Under the Settee* and *Waiting for the Telegram*, both written originally for Thora Hird (your own shortlist of two would probably be the same as ours), we came smack up against the new reality. No amount of social distancing would make us comfortable about asking actors over eighty to get in a car and drive to Elstree, and it soon emerged that the BBC had a temporary rule excluding anyone over seventy. One day, I'd like to return to the shortlist and complete the *Talking Heads* boxed set.

★

We had twelve actors and a schedule, though it had put on a week since Piers floated the idea that we could get going within three. With two to go, we realised we'd never get it all together in time, so we settled on 27 April as the first day of our shoot, which – given that Piers had first called me on 26 March – still seemed improbably soon.

I spent almost all of April staring at my laptop. So did much of the rest of the world, or at least those lucky enough to have co-workers, or friends, or family. I struggle to think of times when the screen felt preferable to being there in the flesh. How do you respond to a film set if you can't stand in the middle of it? How do you know these rooms are where the sole protagonist of your drama might live? How can you imagine where she might sit, cook, sleep, if you can't put yourself where she does the living?

'You can't,' would have been my answer when Simon Bowles started to send iPad shots of the many sets available to us at Elstree. Alone among the team we'd assembled, he was allowed to go there. He was shown around by India Smith, a designer on *EastEnders* who became our supervising art director: just the two of them picking their way through sets that usually throng with actors, crew, and customers of the Queen Vic.

I'm not enough of a regular viewer to know who lives where but, at first glance, none of them lives in the kind of places that the twelve subjects of *Talking Heads* might inhabit. And there was no question of substantially redecorating or refurnishing any of them: nothing could be done that couldn't be carried out by one man and a trolley, no furniture moved that took two people to lift, no repainting, no reupholstery.

'We're stuck with Albert Square?' I asked Simon.

He was relentlessly upbeat. 'We have to celebrate *EastEnders*,' he said. 'For those who watch it, there'll be pleasure in seeing new characters in occupation of the houses they know so well.'

Simon and India then set about making what transformations they could, hanging new pictures, clearing shelves and replacing furniture. Some of the furniture was simply too big to move. Susan, in *Bed Among the Lentils*, has the same green velvet three-piece suite as Albert Square's Phil Mitchell, though she has a different dining table and she's acquired a small piano (from the *EastEnders* prop and furniture store). I can't pretend that the house looks much like the vicarage of Alan's imagination. There's no Aga in the kitchen, for a start; there isn't one in the entire Borough of Walford as far as I know, and so instead of snoozing beside her Aga, Susan dozes off on the sofa, and I doubt anyone notices. (And in defence of the Mitchell residence, even in the 1980s the Church of England was busy moving its vicars into modest houses down the road from the parish church, so it could sell its vicarages and rectories to bankers and lawyers rich enough to do them up and keep an Aga running.)

We improvised. If I'd been starting from scratch, Gwen in *An Ordinary Woman* would have lived in an ordinary semi on an ordinary cul-de-sac in an ordinary new-build estate. As it is, she lives in the flat above the Queen Vic, though I think it's pretty well disguised, not just by Simon and India, but as much by director of photography Zac Nicholson's lighting. Soaps have to be lit and shot at speed. There's a permanent lighting rig hanging above all the *EastEnders* sets. Zac lit them – and, more importantly, the actors – as he would a movie, shot by shot, with meticulous planning and immense imagination, and as a result even the *EastEnders* regulars were astonished by the transfiguration.

It was Sue Mather, the *EastEnders* line producer, who suggested that during our twelve-day shoot, instead of one *Talking Head* per day, we filmed two at a time, on different stages with different directors, and used the intervening days to set up and technically rehearse every shot with stand-ins, so that by the time the actors came in to do their *Talking Head*, every minute of their day could be devoted to capturing their performances. Movies aren't made this

17

way: film crews descend on a location, trailers are pulled into position, and movie stars spend much of the day waiting in them for the set to be readied and lit. At the end of the day, the caravan moves on. It's almost certainly the best use of a movie crew's time, so even though Sue's technical-rehearsal days were invaluable, I can't claim that it's a lesson I'll take from the lockdown world into the real world when it finally returns.

The least likely to survive of lockdown innovations is the Zoom rehearsal. There is no future in it whatsoever. It would never have occurred to me that it was possible to work with an actor without being in the room: human contact is a prerequisite. We all managed because there was no alternative. There was no alternative for family or close friends either but, for all of us, video contact was better than nothing, though nothing like enough.

Which isn't to say that my Zoom rehearsals with Monica Dolan on *The Shrine* (the untitled *Talking Head* had acquired a title), Sarah Lancashire on *An Ordinary Woman* (once *Phèdre*), and Lesley Manville on *Bed Among the Lentils* weren't enjoyable, exciting or productive. They were all three phenomenally focused and imaginative. I sat behind my desk; they sat at their desks or kitchen tables.

There was no question of rehearsing anything except the text, and it was fortunate that none of the *Talking Heads* requires much in the way of movement. Still, it would have been nice to say: 'Shall we try her putting a pie in the oven after she says that?' As it was, I had to say: 'Now she puts a pie in the oven', and neither Sarah nor I knew whether it was a good idea until the pie sat on the kitchen table with the camera rolling. But pies are beside the point: the drama in *Talking Heads* is in the telling of the story, so over the many hours we spent staring at each other on our screens, we were able to get the most important part of the work done.

★

Like all the best writers, Alan creates a world that operates according to its own rules and seems at the same time to be a reflection of reality. He is as distinctly himself as Dickens, or Tennessee Williams, or Elena Ferrante, and like them he seems to be holding the mirror up to somewhere very specific. But Tennessee Williams is no more confined by New Orleans than Elena Ferrante is by Naples or Dickens by London, and it would be as much a mistake to pigeon-hole *Talking Heads* as the work of a Yorkshire writer. It's true that most of the plays are rooted in Yorkshire, but they are the perfect distillation both of Alan's chief concerns as a writer and of his style.

Alan's music is entirely his own and a lot of the rehearsal process is taken up with discovering his rhythms, line by line. Even when he seems to be writing in an explicitly Yorkshire voice, he's actually using speech patterns of his own invention that require more in the way of empathy with his characters than in expertise with a particular accent. He's never keen on actors putting on voices, insists that none of the *Talking Heads* is written in what he calls '*broad* Yorkshire', and when pressed will admit that some of the words he uses might not even be words. Lorna, in *The Shrine*, wonders what happened to the avocado, mozzarella and tomato sandwiches, probably 'wenged in a hedge somewhere, else fed to the ducks'. Monica Dolan wanted to know what 'wenged' meant. We both did internet searches and came up with nothing.

'It means "chucked",' said Alan when I called him. 'I'm not sure, but it may have been made up by my father. He often made up words. "Splother" is another, meaning fuss or to-do. I can remember my father being furious because he thought the neighbour had wenged some dog dirt over the fence, so he wenged it straight back. Change it to "chucked" if you like.' (We did.)

At our directors' Zoom meetings, we talked about how much period detail was needed for the older *Talking Heads*. Some of them seemed to be written in a manner of speech that has disappeared, which suggested they would be best served by a specific period setting. In fact, the vernacular of Alan's world has always been a mash-up of the way his parents spoke, the way people speak now, and his own innate sense of what's worth speaking in the first place. Although the two new *Talking Heads* – *The Shrine* and *An Ordinary Woman* – were written more than thirty years after the first six, Lorna and Gwen speak something like the same language as Miss Ruddock in *A Lady of Letters*, or even, though she's of an entirely different class, Muriel in *Soldiering On*.

Harriet Walter, who plays Muriel this time round, wondered why Alan writes posh so well.

I decided to wing it. 'He was very close to Deborah, Duchess of Devonshire.' (He was her friend, but only towards the end of her life.)

'That might explain it,' said Harriet, unconvinced.

'I could write posh before I could write anything else,'

said Alan, when I asked him the same question. 'I've no idea why.'

I'll have another go at answering: all writers are influenced as much by what they've read as by what they see around them. Alan is in the great tradition of English dramatists, who make what sounds good sound right.

Rudge, the dullest and sportiest of the History Boys, gets into Christ Church, Oxford.

'How come?' asks his astonished teacher.

Rudge explains he has family connections: his dad was a college servant there in the 1950s.

'Mind you,' he continues, 'I did all the other stuff like Stalin was a sweetie and Wilfred Owen was a wuss. They said I was plainly someone who thought for himself and just what the college rugger team needed.'

The real Rudge, if he existed, would never be able to come up with two sentences so witty, so perfectly weighted, so targeted on the big laugh at the end. But a good actor (Russell Tovey, originally) can both get the laugh and never let you doubt for a moment that the real Rudge not only exists but could speak in no other way.

And like almost everyone in Alan's plays, Rudge is written from Rudge's own point of view. Alan often invites you to imagine yourself in the predicaments of people you'd run a mile from if you met them. They might often be blind to themselves (though Rudge isn't, which is why Alan was particularly fond of him) but they are always worth your time. Often they cross the line of decency and are prey to desires that for the best of reasons our society condemns. Among the *Talking Heads* are people who sexually assault children, send poison-pen letters, steal, make porn, accept money for sexual services, shield a serial killer, make incestuous advances on a fifteen-year-old boy. The moral framework that would criminalise many of them is never questioned but neither is their humanity. Here's what it's like to be me, say the *Talking Heads*. 'It's the one bit of my life that feels right,' says the paedophile about the sound of a playground full of children, 'and it's the bit that's wrong.'

The three *Talking Heads* that I directed are quintessentially Bennett. In *Bed Among the Lentils*, the vicar's wife Susan is witheringly funny about the ridiculous people who besiege her absurd husband. By the end of these monologues, you feel you've met a large cast of supporting characters – the vicar, his fan club, the bishop – so vivid is the way they are described by the one person in front of the camera. But although she's surrounded by them,

23

Susan is – like all the *Talking Heads*, maybe like all of us, certainly like many of us during the 2020 lockdown – painfully alone. She is made happy for the first time in her life by a young Indian grocer, Mr Ramesh. He invites her into his bed, and she says she finally understands what the fuss is about. But there are many stories she can't bring herself to admit, and they are pitifully clear to the rest of us. She's an alcoholic. Everyone knows she's an alcoholic. Most distressing of all, and what she never says, is that for a brief shining moment she finds love, and we know all along that it won't last. *Talking Heads* are the acknowledged masterpieces of their genre – television monologue – partly because they ask the audience to work out the real story for themselves.

Another mark of their status as dramatic classics is that they turn out to be capable of total reinvention by great actors. I can't pretend it didn't occur to me that Maggie Smith might have had the last word on *Bed Among the Lentils* in 1988. There is no actor whom I revere or love more than Maggie, and her performance as Susan is indelible. But that's the point: it's Maggie's Susan that is indelible, which doesn't mean that Susan – like any classic role, Cleopatra, say, or Arkadina – can't be made into something else entirely. Lesley Manville, heartbreaking and hilarious, says the same lines as Maggie Smith, but she finds as much new in Susan as she did in Ibsen's Mrs Alving.

*The Shrine* and *An Ordinary Woman*, published in this book, receive introductions from the writer himself, so need nothing from me. But I can't help pointing out that in both of them we experience the same agony as we experience with the vicar's wife: we can see the way things are going long before Lorna or Gwen do. 'He's got a girlfriend,' we long to shout at Gwen, the way we want to shout, 'Iago planted the handkerchief.' But the great dramatists imagine what it's like to be unable to put a halt to the kind of passions that lead to disaster. Some of them even find humour there, though in that department Alan Bennett is the superior of Racine, who wrote *Phèdre*, the play that inspired *An Ordinary Woman*, and who never knowingly landed a laugh.

*

Four weeks to the day after Piers Wenger first called, I finally went to Elstree and met Zac Nicholson and Jacqueline Durran. Jacqueline was knee-deep in eBay deliveries. I had to wait a little longer to meet Simon Bowles in the flesh: by the time we started filming, he was self-isolating with his family because one of them had had to pay a visit to A&E. He emerged halfway through the shoot.

I'm aware now that the next three weeks were convivial in a way that very few were lucky enough to enjoy during lockdown. There were around thirty people, split between two sound stages, occasionally interrupted by cries of 'Two metres, guys! Two metres!' Most of the BBC Studios team were *EastEnders* regulars. The two first assistant directors – Steve Roberts and Julie Sykes – made sure that every day was completed as scheduled. They also kept an instinctively tactile group of people from ever getting within touching distance of each other. Social-distancing protocols that were about to become familiar throughout the world of work were a small price to pay for the privilege of being allowed to make something.

I assumed when we started that it would be impossible to deliver all twelve *Talking Heads* as planned. Somebody, surely, would be unable to turn up, or have to leave early. But everyone stayed healthy. True, most of the people credited at the end of every *Talking Head* never left their homes, but those that did followed the rules and we made seven hours of film.

The first two *Talking Heads* to shoot were *The Shrine* and *Nights in the Gardens of Spain*. I hovered uneasily outside the dressing rooms of Monica Dolan and Tamsin Greig to say good morning. I told Monica that it was nice to meet her after working with her so intimately for so many hours. Tamsin and her director, Marianne Elliott, were old friends from the National Theatre. We all hugged ourselves in an awkward approximation of what theatre people do when they see each other. I finished *The Shrine* a few minutes early, so I went over to the stage where Tamsin and Marianne were shooting. They were onto their last scene: a Spanish patio on a hot night. *EastEnders* had nothing suitable to offer, so Simon and India had put a few terracotta planters in front of some garden trellis in a corner of the studio and Zac had done the rest. It was freezing cold, and Tamsin was dressed for the Mediterranean, and I've no idea why she wasn't shivering. Her teeth chattered between takes. Later on, they added the cicadas. That's how it's always done, and nobody complained.

I'd seen enough of Monica in her own kitchen to know how moving she'd be when finally given the chance to occupy Lorna's. All three of the *Talking Heads* I directed start in the kitchen: they might be epic in emotional scope, but they are domestic in their setting. All the kitchens were fitted out originally for very similar houses in Albert Square. That they seem different is, of course, a tribute to the work of everyone behind the camera, but chiefly it's down to the extraordinary work going on in front of it. Monica Dolan had, in around three weeks, not just learned a long solo text but absorbed it, used it to create a devastating portrait of grief, and through it told a story about how unknowable even those closest to us always turn out to be. I was never in the kitchen to watch her live: only the camera operator Ian Adrian shared the room with her, occasionally joined by John Brady the sound boom operator, though sound was more usually recorded on an enormous Fisher boom that was manoeuvred from outside the set and extended over the top of it. But I watched in awe on the monitor.

Over the next twelve days, every one of the actors came to the set with a character conceived in profound depth, all of them capable of delivering long uninterrupted takes (sometimes twelve minutes), and all of them in absolute control of the Bennett music. They did their own hair and make-up, under Naomi's supervision. They saw many of their costumes only minutes before they went on set. They arrived at around seven in the morning, the camera rolled shortly after eight, and by seven in the evening they were on their way home.

'What do I do now, with all these lines I've learned?' was the parting shot from more than one of them.

I'd never met Jodie Comer, miraculous as Lesley in *Her Big Chance*, or Rochenda Sandall, terrifying as the wounded Margery in *The Outside Dog*. I met Maxine Peake for the first time when she arrived with her irresistible Miss Fozzard, and said goodbye to her minutes after she'd escaped her house in a canary-yellow coat, in the happiest ending of any of the *Talking Heads* (she's discovered sex work and she's off to trample on her chiropodist's bottom). I've never worked with Martin Freeman but, watching him patrol Dot Cotton's bedroom as Graham in *A Chip in the Sugar*, it was impossible to imagine that Alan wrote the part for himself.

Day by day, it became clear to me how detailed the work had been between the actors and their directors, and how individual the directors' work was with the camera. Some of them had never directed for film or television, but with the support of Zac Nicholson and the camera operators Ian Adrian and Matt Hart, they seemed effortlessly to establish the right relationship between the subject of each *Talking*

*Head* and the viewer. And all of the collaborations between actor and director led to performances that took me by surprise when I finally caught up with what they'd been doing together on the day they shot.

Lucian Msamati's unruffled normality as Wilfred in *Playing Sandwiches*, his refusal to acknowledge the harm he does, seduces the audience into a kind of complicity until the full horror becomes unavoidable. Kristin Scott Thomas as Celia in *The Hand of God* is such enjoyable company, so persuasive in her estimation of her own perspicacity, that you happily go along with her malevolent little frauds until you realise, long before she does, that she's been had. And you end up feeling sorry for her. Harriet Walter's stoicism as Muriel in *Soldiering On*, and her blindness to what's going on around her, are representative of the emotional illiteracy of an entire class. She sometimes allows herself crushing glimpses into the depth of her own misery. As Miss Ruddock in *A Lady of Letters*, Imelda Staunton sits at her front window, watching. There is no stopping her vindictive interference in the lives of others, until – in a single pause – her whole life seems to fall over a cliff. Then, almost as quickly, she turns her ruin into her salvation. It's an extraordinary piece of acting.

The three performances I knew best were, of course, the three I directed. *An Ordinary Woman* was the final *Talking Head* to wrap, so I said my last goodbye to Sarah Lancashire on the same day I met her properly for the first time. We shot her monologue in something like story order, though we saved the hospital scene, as the set was on a separate stage. She started the day as an ordinary mum in a charming family comedy and ended it utterly broken. The quiet intensity of her descent was sometimes almost impossible to watch. Between takes she was as elated by the quality of the writing as I was by her performance.

After Sarah left, I joined a bewildered group of new colleagues. Normally we'd go for a drink or have a party to mark the end of a shoot. We hung around for a while on one of the stages and slowly drifted apart.

★

*Talking Heads* require very little editing in the traditional sense. There's no cutting from medium shot to close-up, from one character to another. The directors had to choose the best take of every shot, and how quickly to fade to black at the beginning and end of each of them. All twelve films were picture-locked within two days. It took another three weeks to complete grading and sound. It was a scramble, but for me at least it felt like a holiday after spending every waking hour on pre-production and production.

For the composer George Fenton, it was a period of astounding achievement. George was the only member of the team, apart from Alan himself, who had been involved in the original series. He's composed the music for all of Alan's films, and indeed mine. Back in March, he was one of the first people I called, to ask if he'd do them again. He paused for quite a long time, which he often does, so I wasn't alarmed.

'I won't be able to leave the house,' he said.

'I know. But you have a studio there.'

'I won't be able to get hold of any musicians. Or sound engineers.'

'Can't you do all that yourself? It could all be piano, couldn't it?' I thought I wouldn't let him tell me, as he often does, how terrible a pianist he is, because I know he isn't. 'You can send it all through on an MP3 or something, can't you?' I tried to sound more knowledgeable than I am.

A long pause.

'Nick, there must be more than seventy different music cues.'

In the end, George wrote seventy-eight cues, plus the front- and end-credit sequences. Early on, I introduced him to the other directors on one of our Zoom calls. George is the least dogmatic person I've ever met. He will always give a director or a writer room to have their own ideas, or to ask for something different from what he's composed. I knew that all the directors would want to talk to him about what kind of music their individual *Talking Head* would require, and I also knew that we needed to make a collective decision about a musical language that would unify the series. And, more to the point, we needed to give George a brief that he could achieve in the time available.

'But don't talk about what's possible and impossible, George,' I said to him. 'Don't tell them they'll be getting second best. Tell them simple isn't just more practical; tell them it's perfect. Tell them solo piano will work better than anything else. They know who you are! They'll believe you!'

I felt like a boxing coach. George took notes on the back of an envelope, told the directors that what he proposed was the best possible music for *Talking Heads* under any circumstances and, as it turned out, all the directors were overjoyed with the music he wrote, performed and recorded by himself in the studio across the yard from his house. And he went much further than solo piano, though everything you hear – keyboards, guitar, clarinet, cello – is played by George, or at least the sounds are created by George.

He sent the first demo for *The Shrine* on 3 May and by the end of May he'd delivered the lot. 'The interesting and tiring part', he wrote to me later, 'was getting my head round three monologues a week – resetting or restarting the writing process twelve times with seven directors, six of whom I'd never met (and still haven't!) though they were all, without exception, charming and helpful.'

It's one more dinner of which I feel cheated: when the *Talking Heads* directors get to meet their composer. We'll have it one day. Maybe we'll invite the writer too. They'd all quite like to meet him.

*

*Talking Heads* was delivered on 5 June, ten weeks and a day after Piers Wenger first called with the idea. Someday, the lockdown will be a distant memory. Maybe the most useful part of this story will be that there was once a twelve-part series that, for some weird reason, took only ten weeks from conception to delivery. ('So why the hell are we

34

waiting for a green light on this script three years after we handed it in?' I can hear future film-makers wail.)

As I write, I am once again the top of nobody's list to make anything for television, and my attention has switched fully to the perilous future of the performing arts, which was never far from the front of my mind during the ten-week foray into film. I yearn for the day that audiences pour back into the foyer of the Bridge Theatre, and I grieve for the theatres that might never open their doors again, and for the performing artists whose lives are on hold and whose careers might never recover. I was lucky. I got to make a series for the BBC. I hope a lot of people get to sit on their sofas and watch it.

But much, much more than that, I hope that somebody will one day pick up this book in a second-hand bookshop (assuming they still exist), leaf through the introduction, and vaguely remember that there was once a terrible virus that brought nearly everything to a halt. And I hope she buys the book, because two short plays by Alan Bennett will always be worth having. And then she joins her friends in the bar next door, and together they walk through crowded streets to the theatre.

June 2020

AN ORDINARY WOMAN

*Puisque je retrouve un ami si fidèle*
*Ma fortune va prendre une face nouvelle*

The opening line of Racine's *Phèdre*, and almost the only thing I remember from School Certificate French with Mr Durling at Leeds Modern School, sometime in 1950. Mr Durling was fond of declaiming (with a lot of spit) the verse of Racine, though I don't recall him ever spelling out its shocking plot, in which Phèdre falls for her stepson Hippolytus. I say shocking, but though I was far from being a sophisticated boy I don't remember being shocked at all; indeed, I was surprised it didn't happen more often.

Not that it did happen, of course, that was the point but the religious horror of the set-up was lost on me. I was in love with a boy two forms below mine and there would have been religious horror at that, had anybody known but me (including him). So, if I identified with anyone in this family romance it certainly wasn't Hippolytus but his stepmother.

This was a state school in the 1940s where divorce among the parents – and the stepchildren that often accompanies it – was rare. Did mothers experience a twinge of illicit affection for their stepsons, nobody ever said, but nobody ever said much about sex around me anyway; I wasn't that kind of boy. Phèdre was cross because her stepson Hippolytus had vowed himself to perpetual virginity. Pious though I was, I hadn't gone that far, though there was so little happening I might as well.

Around this time, Mr Durling took 5A into town and the Tower Cinema to see Leeds's first post-war French film, Marcel Carné's *Les Enfants du paradis*. Quite what was going on I wasn't sure, but back at school Mr Durling lectured the largely clueless class about the blindness and disease that awaited us fifteen-year-old boys did we model ourselves on the circus folk of provincial France. I can only presume he'd read as little of *Phèdre* as we had or, veering so close to incest, it could never have become a set book.

Seventy years after I studied the play, *Phèdre* still seems to me a cop-out, and in *An Ordinary Woman* the mother falls not for the relatively easy option of a stepson but for her own flesh and blood, with the situation predictably insoluble besides being intolerable for all concerned.

Though all toga'd up a few years ago at the National Theatre, Helen Mirren and Dominic Cooper were moving in their desperation, but these days murder is not an option. As a young man, I used to pretend I wasn't part of the human race. That's one solution. Or be a writer.

Alan Bennett

May 2020

*An Ordinary Woman* was first broadcast on BBC1
on 23 June 2020

| | |
|---:|:---|
| *Gwen* | Sarah Lancashire |
| *Director* | Nicholas Hytner |
| | |
| *Casting Director* | Robert Sterne |
| *Music Composed by* | George Fenton |
| *Line Producer* | Susan Mather |
| *Associate Producer* | Dinah Wood |
| *Co-Producer* | Steve Clark Hall |
| *Hair and Make-Up Designer* | Naomi Donne |
| *Costume Designer* | Jacqueline Durran |
| *Editor* | Stephen Young |
| *Production Designer* | Simon Bowles, BFDG |
| *Director of Photography* | Zac Nicholson, BSC |
| *Executive Producers* | Medwyn Jones, Andrew Leveson, Nick Starr, Piers Wenger |
| *Produced by* | Nicholas Hytner and Kevin Loader |

*An ordinary kitchen. Gwen, a middle-aged woman, talks to the camera.*

He pulled up his trousers.

'You are nice to me,' he said. 'I couldn't have shown it to anybody else.'

I said, 'Well, I hope you haven't been doing.'

'Oh,' he said. 'Not much chance of that. No demand at the moment.'

He'd come home from school looking a bit down and retreats upstairs to his room and doesn't even bother to raid the fridge, by which I take it something's amiss. He plays his music for a bit and I'm ironing when he comes down barefoot and sits at the table watching me, which is an event in itself. Suddenly he gets up and says, 'Mum, I'm going to show you this, but it'll be the last time you'll ever see it.'

And he undoes his trousers and pulls down his shorts.

He said, 'Now, what's that?'

Well, it was nothing. I couldn't even see where he meant until he points it out, just a bit of a spot. Only it was the other I couldn't get over. I hadn't been keeping track and I don't know when I last saw it exactly, but he can't have been much more than twelve. And he's only fifteen now but you wouldn't know.

He said, 'Are you sure?'

I said, 'Michael. It's a spot, love, that's all it is', and I got him some stuff to put on.

He gets his trousers up sharp.

He said, 'Don't tell Dad.'

'Why should I tell Dad? Why should I tell Dad anything?'

'And don't tell our Maureen.'

'As if,' I said (which is what he's always saying).

'I don't want my private parts mulled over by my sister.'

He's getting some pie from the fridge.

I said, 'Wash your hands.'

He said, 'You said it was nothing.'

I said, 'It is nothing but wash your hands.'

★

It's an aerodrome we go to, disused. We shouldn't but he's only fifteen so it would be illegal anywhere else, and I'm not altogether sure it's legal there, but it's off the road and he's desperate to start driving. His dad's not keen but he doesn't have the patience to teach him anyway.

I nearly killed him though today. There was a lad gunning his motorbike about and Michael nearly went into him, scraped him. It was my fault. I should have been looking in the mirror. He scarcely touched us, this lad, and just belted off, only I had my hand gripping Michael's leg I was so shocked. And he was trembling. He said, 'Mum, let go my leg.' I said, 'I hope it hasn't scratched the bodywork.' He said, 'It's my bodywork I'm bothered about, let go my leg.' Anyway, there was only a tiny mark on the bumper. I couldn't hardly see it, only I said I'd tell Dad it was me that was driving.

I'd brought a flask, so we sat there on this runway having some coffee. I said, shouted actually, with having his music on, 'Is this what they call "quality time"?'

And he nods, though whether at me or the music I couldn't tell. And then he's looking at his phone.

Later on, Maureen saw me checking the bumper. She said, 'Is that a scratch?'

'No, it fucking well isn't,' Michael said. 'And anyway Mum was driving.'

He winks at me. And I wink back, only I can't wink so just screwed my face up.

He looks more than fifteen.

Thinking about it afterwards, I didn't see the bike because I was looking at Michael's hands on the wheel and thinking how much nicer they are than my hands.

★

'John Lennon,' Michael said. 'That's the first thing Mum remembers, him being shot.'

I said, 'Is it?'

'Well, that's what you told me.'

Maureen is doing her homework. 'It's Miss Macaulay,' said Michael. '*Milestones*. We did it two years ago.'

'It's Mum I have to ask,' said Maureen. 'Not you.'

'It's true, love,' I said. 'I do remember that.'

'I don't think Miss Macaulay is into the Beatles. Who else got shot? Martin Luther King. Do you remember that? Because that's more up her street.'

'That', said his lordship, scratching his armpit, 'is because she's a lesbian.'

'She never is,' Maureen said. 'She's got a friend in Lawnswood.'

'Sure,' says Michael. 'A lady friend.'

I said, 'Stop it, the pair of you, or you'll do your homework upstairs.' I can't bear it when he starts bickering. One minute he's so grown up, the next he's back to being ten years old.

'I'm sorry, precious', and he puts on his caring voice and starts stroking her arm.

'Don't touch me,' Maureen says. 'Most sex crimes are committed in the family. Anybody touches me, that's a crime.'

'I shouldn't worry,' he says. 'Nobody's going to.'

'What?'

'Touch you.'

'Nobody's going to touch you either.'

'Oh, really?' he says. 'How do you know they haven't already?'

I put my hands over my ears and really lost it.

'Stop it. Stop it. Leave each other alone.' That shut them both up and she goes off upstairs, crying as usual.

I said, 'If anybody does touch you . . .'

He said, 'What's this "anybody"? Do you mean a girl? Because it's not going to be anybody else.'

I said, 'Promise me, if a girl does touch you . . . I mean, properly . . . you won't tell me.'

He says, 'Don't worry. I won't. Why?'

'Because I don't want to know.'

'Anyway,' he says, 'they won't.'

I said, 'They will. They'll be all over you.'

'I hate these type of conversations,' he says, and charges off upstairs. Whereupon Maureen comes down, having been listening.

'I'll tell you,' she says.

'Tell me what?'

'If anything's going on, with him.'

'I don't want you to tell me. I don't want you to tell me anything. Though you must tell me if anything happens with you.'

'It won't,' she says. 'I put people off.'

At which point Dad arrives home and we send out for a curry. I let them get on with it, only Michael says, 'Are you not having any?'

'No,' I say. 'It doesn't always agree with me. I'll just have a bit of cheese and an apple.'

'More for us,' says Dad.

Later I'm stacking the dishwasher while Dad is next door watching the news. Suddenly Michael says, 'Mum. I know what's going on. I'm fifteen. I know what's happening.'

I said, 'Well, I'm forty-two and I don't. What is going on?'

'You're having an affair. There are all the signs. New hairdo. Lipstick.'

I said, 'There's no law against lipstick.'

'And slimming,' he said.

I laughed.

He said, 'It's not the menopause?'

I said, 'It's a bit soon for that. Anyway, what do you know about the menopause?'

He said, 'We did it in Social Hygiene. Anyway, that's a relief.'

'Why?'

'Well, I don't go for all that father-and-son shit but I'd still have felt sorry for Dad.'

He wanted his shirt washing. I said, 'There's a clean one upstairs.'

Only he likes this one.

'Stand by,' he says and takes it off and I put it on Quick Wash.

I said, 'You've got lovely skin.'

He said, 'So they tell me.'

I said, 'Who? Girls?'

He said, 'Well, not boys.'

He said, 'There's nothing wrong, is there?'

I said, 'No.'

'Because you're thinner.'

I said, 'That's good, isn't it?'

He said, 'I like you the way you are.'

'Fat, you mean?'

'No. Comfortable. Adam's mother's got thin. It's painful. I don't know why they do it. What does Dad think?'

'Oh, he won't have noticed.'

He put his hands on his head and watches me while I ironed his shirt. I looked away.

He said, 'Did you look away then?'

I said, 'No.'

He said, 'I look all right, though.'

I said, 'You look lovely.'

He said, 'I wish somebody else thought so.'

'Who?'

'Anybody.'

Then Maureen has to go and come down because I haven't ironed her PE stuff. Michael said, 'It was lovely till you turned up', and clears off to his room.

(*Pause.*)

Fifteen, so I suppose he wanks.

I lie in bed and his bed's just on the other side of the wall, but I never hear anything.

★

He doesn't smell. He doesn't smell at all. His T-shirts feel a bit stale and they smell of him but they don't smell. I didn't think this could happen. I thought there was something, genes or something, that gave you immunity. I can see how you could quite easily fall for your stepson, say, somebody who's joined the family, but not your own child. I thought that was inbred. I'm lying there on his bed with all his things piled on top of me. I think I was actually chewing his T-shirt when I heard something downstairs and it's our Maureen back from school early. Asbestos in the art room. I manage to get the clothes all into the basket and into our bedroom before she comes upstairs. She said, 'Why is our Michael's door open?' I said, 'I'm getting the washing. Have you got anything?' She said, 'I thought you did it yesterday. Why are you all undone at the front?' I said, 'It's just something I took off to put in the wash, what do you want for your tea?'

53

Later on I went over to see Louisa. She still smokes so we adjourned to the end of the garden, and I said how nice Michael was being.

She said, 'They are at that age. Just before they take off. Ricky's the same. I can't look at him sometimes, I fancy him that much.' And she laughs, as if this is the most normal thing in the world. I said, 'Does he know?'

'That I fancy him? Course. I tell him. I tell him all the time.'

'And doesn't he mind?' She said, 'No. It was him that said it, he caught me looking at him out of the bath and he said, "You fancy me, don't you?" I said, "Don't flatter yourself."'

'But he was suited, you could see.'

'Michael wouldn't be,' I said. 'Though he tells me everything.'

'No, he doesn't, love. They never do.'

Coming away, I wish I hadn't said anything. She makes it seem so dirty.

I could never tell him.

Only I have to tell somebody.

★

I'm not religious but I thought I could go and see the vicar, only I got off on the wrong foot because a woman comes to the door with her marigolds on. I said, 'Is the vicar in?'

She said, 'Yes.'

I said, 'Could I see him?'

She said, 'It's not a him. It's a her. Come in. I'm just making some jam.'

She doesn't have a collar on and I thought with her being a woman it might be easier, only to begin with I just sat there not knowing where to start.

She said, 'How can I help you?' Glued to the Aga.

I said, 'I'm not sure you can. It's my son.'

She said, 'Has he done something wrong?'

I said, 'No. Nobody's done anything wrong. Are you sure it's not burning?'

She said, 'It needs a good rolling boil. It's blackberry. Is that a good rolling boil?'

I said, 'I don't know. We generally have bought jam. I've always wanted an Aga.'

'Yes,' she said. 'It's a godsend, though I suppose I shouldn't say that.'

I said, 'Why?'

'With being a vicar. Godsend. How old is he, your son?'

'Fifteen. Though he looks older.'

'They all look older now. I've got a partner. Didn't you used to work at the library?'

'I did.'

'Sad, that going.'

'It is,' I said. 'I miss it. The thing is . . . I love my son.'

'Well, he's your son. I hope you do.'

'No. I mean . . . I'm in love with him. Only I'm just an ordinary woman.'

'Nobody's ordinary in the sight of God.'

That didn't seem to me to get us any further, so I said, 'Nothing's happened. We haven't done anything.' (I didn't tell her I'd thought about it.) 'He doesn't even know.'

'Maybe . . .' – and she has another squint at the jam – 'Maybe you should tell him.'

I said, 'He wouldn't understand.'

She said, 'People have more to them than one gives them credit for.'

I said, 'He's not people. He's fifteen.'

She said, 'I suppose it's no good telling you that God would call it a sin?'

I said, 'How's the jam doing?'

She said, 'It's a crush. It'll pass. Give it time. It's like bringing him up and living together in the family . . . you do have a husband?'

I said, yes, I did.

She said, 'Only living in close proximity together bestows a kind of protective coating on members of the family, so that in normal circumstances they don't fall for each other, and somehow your protective coating has gone missing. Why would that be, do you think?'

I knew how it started but I wasn't going to tell her that.

As I'm going, she says, 'Does your husband know?'

I said, 'No.'

She said, 'Don't you think you should share it with him?'

I said, 'Share? No. Good luck with the jam.'

Afterwards I went and sat in the church.

I don't feel . . . I don't feel I'm even entitled to this . . . well . . . passion. It's lofty. Shakespearean. A man came to talk to us at the library once and he said love transformed, so that even the most ordinary people could become . . . epic, I think it was.

But . . . I'm just an ordinary woman.

★

I can't get over it. Fifteen. *Fifteen*.

Where did it come from, this understanding?

Where did he acquire it? Not from me. And not from his dad.

Is this Social Hygiene? I can't think so.

Only it's happened.

Though nothing's happened really.

Adam had been round, both of them upstairs playing on the computer.

Maureen came down, listening at the door as usual, saying that they're watching porn, only I said it was none of her business . . . it's only a phase anyway.

When eventually they do come down, I make them some French toast.

Except Maureen says, 'I expect you've worked up an appetite.'

Michael takes no notice, just tells her to fuck off, but Adam's an only child and he's not used to sisters and goes scarlet and says, 'We weren't doing anything, Mrs Fedder', and our Michael groans and tells him to forget it.

When he's gone Michael says, 'You are good, Mum.'

I said, 'Why, what have I done now?'

He said, 'Not taking on. We weren't even watching anything, only Adam had brought round a new game. You're
lovely, though, Mum. You never get shocked. Poor Adam
was creased.'

'No point in being shocked anyway,' I said. 'You know
it all.'

'Well,' he said. 'Not quite all.'

And he looks at me, really hard. And I thought, 'He knows.'

I said, 'No. Not quite. Though there's something I've
been wanting to say.'

'Feel free,' he said. 'I might have something to tell you.'

And he puts his hand over mine and leaves it there.

At which point, of course, Dad comes home from work
and he takes his hand off mine really sharp, I mean as if it's
red hot.

So he's hiding it, too.

Dad didn't notice but we're going to have to be so careful.

But I'm so happy.

It doesn't seem real.

★

I thought I was on safe ground.

Otherwise, I wouldn't have spoken.

59

I said, 'But what was it you were going to tell me yesterday? I said I had something to tell you . . .'

'You sure did . . .'

'. . . but you had something to tell me.'

'Oh, that I'd got a girlfriend. What does it matter now?' (*Pause.*)

He says he's still trying to get his head round it.

'When you say "love", you don't mean sex and stuff?'

I should have said, 'Yes. Yes. That's just what I do mean.'

Only I said, 'No. It depends.'

'On what?' he says. 'Me being out of my mind? You're my *mother.*'

And suddenly he dashes to the back door and is sick on the step.

He comes back saying, 'Isn't it against the law? It's one of the few things that is.'

I said, 'Loving isn't against the law.'

And he just pushed me, really hard, so that I went over on my bad knee.

He said, 'Are you all right?'

I nod.

'Oh Christ,' he says and picks me up but . . . it was

touching me, I suppose . . . he screws up his face and pulls away from me as if I'm dirty.

Which I am, I suppose, now. The dirty mother.

The blameless father comes home later on, but nobody puts him in the picture. The dirty mother can't face it and the object of her affection doesn't know how to.

In the end it's Maureen who does it, who's unsurprised.

Sitting at the kitchen table and saying, 'Well, I knew all along.'

'We were so nice and ordinary,' Michael says. 'Now look at us.'

Maureen says, 'I think it's quite interesting.'

(*Pause.*)

I've never known the house so quiet.

★

*Gwen is in bed in hospital, although we don't see any other patients. Her hair is wild, having been washed but not set.*

I never thought I'd land up here, only I've not been sectioned and if I wanted I could walk out tomorrow, but the way I am now one place is much like another. Dad comes and sits, bit wary at first but our Maureen comes all the time. Brings her homework and does it at the bottom of the bed. I've got to like her more now than I used to. Of course, she's got no competition as Michael hasn't been near.

I blame the therapist, Marny her name is. A doctor but just in ordinary clothes. No white coat. Lots of frizzy hair. Because I wasn't in here to begin with. I was at home. I was on tablets and it was miserable but we were managing. Only Marny has a thing about goals, recovery is a journey and all that stuff, and now that Michael has a girlfriend one stage would be if the girlfriend stopped the night.

Not keen and nor was Michael by all accounts. We don't talk much, only he told his dad he thought it was a bit soon and probably they wouldn't do anything anyway. I mean, it's only the other side of the wall.

They reckoned to give me an extra sleeping tablet but if they did it didn't work, and I think Dad was awake too, only he never let on.

Anyway, far from not doing anything, they went on all night and apparently . . . though I don't remember this quite . . . I must have got up in the small hours, found my hairdryer of all things, and started braying on his door. He'd locked it or else I'd've gone in, choose what they were doing. Apparently I was shouting, 'Stop it.' 'Stop it', and the hairdryer broke in my hand and cut me and there was blood all down the door. The girl was hysterical, Dad and Michael shouting at one another, Michael with not a stitch on and Maureen stood at her door taking it all in. 'Family life,' was all she said. Anyway, she had the sense to phone the ambulance. I'd severed a tendon apparently, which they stitched up in A&E before they fetched me in here for assessment.

Assessment being a lot of talking, though not by me. And Dad's not much better, though he tries, bless him. We both of us have to learn to verbalise more, apparently. If we'd verbalised more, Marny says, it probably wouldn't have happened. Now that he's been told it was all some sort of symptom, Michael feels it was at least more respectable. More normal is what he means.

I don't know that I do, because I remember what started it all and I told that to the nice Indian doctor who said that was just the trigger. Some trigger. Lou's been. Blames the therapist. Says lots of women feel the same. Adam's talked to Michael, who claims he understands. He doesn't. He won't understand until he falls for someone inappropriate himself.

I just sit a lot of the time. Once they've got the tablets

sorted out I can go home apparently. Back under the same roof.

★

We're never in the same room, Michael and me. Not on our own anyway. That's not the therapist. That's him. Feels easier, he says. So Dad'll be here, else Maureen, who'll always be here anyway. I don't know whether they've told her to keep me busy but she never lets me alone. She says, 'I can't, Mum. I love you. Have you taken your tablets?'

I asked Marny what the tablets did. She said, 'Well, one thing they do is start to put back your insulation, make you indifferent to one another the way families normally are. Somehow,' she says, 'you lost your mother's insulation, so he stopped being your son and became just a lad.' I said, 'Will he have to take them too?' Only she said, 'No, because he's never lost his protective coating.'

He did come in after school this afternoon with our Maureen in tow. Sits across the room like I'm infectious. I said, 'I'm on tablets now. You can take my hand.' Only he didn't.

He said, 'You mustn't love me, Mum.'

64

'I don't any more,' I said. 'I've told you. I'm on tablets. And I can love you both now.'

'And Dad as well,' said Maureen, holding my hand, 'Just like a proper family.'

Michael got up. He said, 'I won't kiss you.'

I said, 'How many more times. It's all right. I don't feel anything.'

'Best to be on the safe side,' he says, and just blows me one.

Dad thinks I might do away with myself.

He said, 'You must promise me not to do anything silly.'

'Have I ever done anything silly, apart from this?'

Whereas now it's all about forgetting and moving on. Closure.

I'm not saying anything, only I'm not going to forget, choose what they give me.

One of the doctors said, 'You've no business having thoughts like that, a nice middle-aged lady like you.'

But I did.

And (*here her voice breaks*) I do.

Only the more I think about it, the more I think –

I'm just an ordinary woman.

# THE SHRINE

Where a play or a story (or for that matter a poem) comes from isn't always easy to say or particularly desirable. Identifying the source of one's inspiration ('Where do you get your ideas from?') can be dispiriting, with a risk that the idea remains unachieved, the trek from thought to thing a bit of a wasted journey.

With *The Shrine*, though, it's more straightforward: I could go there tomorrow. Homemade memorials, if not quite up to Lorna's makeshift cenotaph, are nowadays a common sight on Britain's roads. Driving by, one scarcely notices them, still less slows down. Which is why Lorna behaves as she does. 'Lest we forget.' Or, as Lorna sees it, 'Lest you forget.'

Buried or commemorated elsewhere in conventional cemeteries, the dead are more permanent attractions. By the roadside, even with the best of intentions, they are only briefly remembered and the floral tributes, the carnations in their cellophane, soon stop coming. The pilgrimage after all is often awkward. 'It's a really nasty corner and they go mad round that bit.' Which is why they are having to make the visit in the first place. 'Do you wonder folks get killed?'

The road with which I am most familiar is the A65. Largely unbypassed, it's the main road from Leeds to the Lake District and is always crowded with coveys of bikers, roosting at intervening towns like Skipton, Settle and Kirkby Londsdale. I no longer drive, though even when I did I scarcely considered myself a motorist and found it hard not to feel threatened by the speed and suddenness of overtaking bikers. Though that isn't the point of the piece.

I'm sure I'm not the first to take note of these wayside memorials and I'm indebted to Mike Harding who has written a poem on the same subject. 'The Shrine' was his title.

Alan Bennett
May 2020

*The Shrine* was first broadcast on BBC1
on 9 July 2020

| | |
|---|---|
| *Lorna* | Monica Dolan |
| *Director* | Nicholas Hytner |
| | |
| *Casting Director* | Robert Sterne |
| *Music Composed by* | George Fenton |
| *Line Producer* | Susan Mather |
| *Associate Producer* | Dinah Wood |
| *Co-Producer* | Steve Clark Hall |
| *Hair and Make-Up Designer* | Naomi Donne |
| *Costume Designer* | Jacqueline Durran |
| *Editor* | Rob Platt |
| *Production Designer* | Simon Bowles, BFDG |
| *Director of Photography* | Zac Nicholson, BSC |
| *Executive Producers* | Medwyn Jones, Andrew Leveson, Nick Starr, Piers Wenger |
| *Produced by* | Nicholas Hytner and Kevin Loader |

*A middle-aged woman, Lorna, sits at a kitchen table.*
*She talks to the camera. Very flat.*


The policeman said, did I want to see where it happened?

I said, 'What good would that do?'

He said, 'It might help towards closure.'

I said, 'Closure? It was only last Sunday. They haven't even had the inquest yet.'

Had his notebook out. Kept ticking stuff off. Said he knew it must be hard but did I want counselling? I said, 'Who does that, the RAC?'

He said, 'That's a no, I take it?'

How long had he had the bike? Could I confirm what cc it was?

*(She shakes her head.)*

He said that they generally put some flowers on the spot where it happened, courtesy of the police. I said they could save their money as he didn't much care for flowers. Only the police apparently do it anyway, as the feeling is that it reminds the public where a tragedy happened, so it's an investment as the flowers are a contribution to road safety and come off the council precept.

Only young. He said it was normally a policewoman only they're shorthanded.

Oh Clifford.

You silly sod.

★

I said, 'Birdwatching? Clifford, you don't need a motorbike to do birdwatching. What's wrong with the car, then we could both go?'

He said, 'We could both go on the bike.'

I said, 'Me on the bike? No fear. Flaming thing.'

I keep thinking about those scrutty police carnations tied to a fence somewhere. They'll just have come from a garage and still be in their cellophane. I hate that. So, if only for the flowers, I thought I ought to put in an appearance. And at least it gets me out of the house.

Well, it's way up the A65 on the other side of Skipton and it took a bit of locating. No flowers on any fence that I could see and I kept getting hooted at for slowing down looking. Only then I saw these skid marks on the verge and there were some flowers on the grass, white, whereas I'd been looking for red, and not carnations, chrysanths. Only

I was lucky because there's a layby opposite and I could put the car in there.

Aught else and it could have been a nice spot. Patch of grass, little bank, some bushes and the odd tree, and in the next field there's sheep and, in the distance, hills. Awful that it was there, but not a bad place. One sheep came over and looked at me. Maybe it came and looked at him.

I sat there on the verge for a bit, cars and lorries thundering past. And bikes, of course. They love that road. It's nowhere but still it's a real place. Or him dying there has made it a place. I'd taken some proper flowers, lilies they were, and I leant them up against the tree. Bark gone, so maybe that was the tree.

Only I'll not go again. It's morbid. And I don't want to make a career out of his grave. Not that it is his grave. It's a copse almost. Except that's what they call a place when there's been a crime there. With it being wet, the bike had churned up the grass and you could follow where it must have skidded and thrown him off. I took a couple of pictures to send to our Eileen in Australia.

Policeman's just called. Inquest been adjourned. Doesn't know why. A backlog was all he said.

Earlier on when I was stood there watching all the cars and lorries, I kept wondering why nobody stopped. Somebody died, after all. But of course they don't stop. Why should they?

Policeman said, did I know what was in his pannier bag?

I said, 'Listen. The bike was his province. Why?'

He said, 'Just filling in the gaps.'

I loved you, Clifford. So why don't I feel anything?

Lonely, I feel that.

★

I found a board and a couple of bricks in the garage and I've made myself a little seat. It's on the side furthest from the road, looking over the field. So in between sessions I go and sit there and watch the sheep . . . I do half an hour at a time, just standing there where the bike came off the road.

Don't look at the traffic or anything passing, just straight ahead. Bearing witness, I suppose, except I wasn't a witness. That was the problem at the inquest . . . no witness. Nobody saw it happen. That's partly why it's been adjourned, apparently. I come twice a week, weather permitting . . . except I'll come in the rain sometimes. No umbrella. Folks do stare at that, standing in the rain.

Not counting my sentry duty, there's lots to do besides. I keep it immaculate and just as it was, clear up any litter . . . because it's shocking the stuff people just chuck on the verge.

It is a grave, after all.

Once upon a time an incident – they keep calling it an incident not an accident – once upon a time somebody dying would give a place a name, earn it a designation.

Clifford's Corner, Biker's End.

Not now. It happens too often for that. This road particularly would be a string of names. A death map. Only what erases it all is traffic, wipes out memory and remembrance. Nobody's actually stopped to ask me but, say they did, that's what I'd say: I'm standing here as a reminder.

I wonder if it was a bird or a badger made him swerve. Because I do see birds. There's a kite comes sometimes, cruel-looking thing. He may have been looking at that.

He was in his leathers, only at the inquest the police said his trousers were open.

That doesn't sound like Clifford.

Some strange flowers there today. Not mine. Nice, I suppose.

★

I've got myself an orange jacket. 'High-vis', they call them. With luck folks will notice me a bit more. The last thing I want to do is blend in. The young policeman stopped today. Parked his Panda in the layby and walked across.

Said, did I have a moment?

I said, 'Well, I've got my schedule to keep up, only don't stand there.'

He said, 'Where?' I said, 'You're right on the tyre tracks. I try to keep them crisp if I can. Out of respect.' He stood on the grass and said, 'Is this all right?' I said, 'I hope you've noticed I've got a safety jacket on.' He said, 'Yes, only . . .'

I said, 'Only what?' He said, 'Well, I can understand where you're coming from, and I can appreciate your need to grieve, only . . . you've started kneeling now, haven't you?'

I said, 'Yes, I do kneel. It makes more of a statement.' He said, 'Yes, only you must see that on your knees and in that jacket you're a real hazard. Drivers notice you. They look.'

I said, 'They're meant to.' He said, 'Yes, only you're an accident waiting to happen.'

I said, 'So do you not want me to wear the jacket, or do you not want me to kneel?'

He said, 'Neither if it's all the same to you. Can't you just make up your mind to move on? People do.'

I said, 'Move on? The inquest hasn't even come out yet.'

He said, 'That's something I want to talk to you about.'

We went and sat on the seat. He said, 'This is nice. Sheep.'

I said, 'Yes. They'd come over if you weren't here. They know me now.'

He took his hat off. 'Did your hubby ever have a passenger? Somebody on the pillion?' I said, 'He didn't know anybody. If anybody was ever going to go on the pillion it would be me. Why?' He said, 'Well, he was carrying a spare crash helmet in his pannier.'

I said, 'I don't know what he carried. He was birdwatching. There can't have been anybody else.'

He said, 'I'm not saying there was. Only . . .' – he was looking at the sheep all this time – '. . . you don't always need anybody else. The autopsy showed he'd just . . .'

I said, 'Just what?'

He said, 'Climaxed.'

I'd never heard it called that.

I said, 'Clifford? No.'

He said, 'It's the speed. They get a kick out of it.'

I said, 'Birdwatchers?'

79

He said, 'Bikers. He was a biker first and a birdwatcher second.'

I said, 'How do you know?'

He said, 'Don't worry. It won't come out. The coroner is very discreet.' He sat for a minute or two.

I said, 'You've got some of the mud on your trousers.' I said, 'I'm still going to kneel, only I won't wear the jacket.' He said, 'That's the stuff', and just pipped his horn as he went off.

The kite came later on, circling round.

More flowers today.

Anemones.

★

What I do now is I meet the police halfway. I either wear the jacket and stand, or don't wear the jacket and kneel. I bring my garden kneelers now and they make it easier.

I'd just done a stint yesterday and was freshening up the tyre treads when somebody roars up on a bike. Doesn't park in the layby but lugs his bike up onto the verge. Another foot and he'd have been right on the place. A cross on the front of his helmet but it's only when he takes it off I realise he's a vicar. Shakes hands. Says he's a vicar first and a biker second.

Only he can't keep still, wanders about all over the grass by the tree, you'd think with him being a vicar he'd be more sensitive. Eventually I make him sit on the seat, where he asks if he can say a prayer. I say, 'It's a bit late for that.' He says, 'Not for him, for you.' He said, 'I bless bikes. I'm the rev who revs. I probably blessed your husband's bike.'

I thought, well, it didn't do him much good, but I didn't say so.

I said, 'Did the police send you?' He said, 'Not specifically.' I said, 'They were trying to make out there'd been somebody on the pillion.' He said, 'Lorna.' (They must have told him that an' all.) 'Lorna. There was someone on the pillion. Jesus was on the pillion. He always is . . . even if we're not riding a bike.'

He asks me how I see it ending.

I say, 'I don't. I'm bearing witness.'

He said, 'What to?'

I said, 'Death.' He said, 'Well, I can't quarrel with that, obviously, but isn't there something more constructive you can do?'

I said, 'Like what?'

'Form a society, say. Get together with others bereaved in the same way. Move on. After all that's what cemeteries are for, not places by the roadside.' He got up. 'Did he hit this tree?'

I said, 'I imagine so. The sheep will have seen it.'

He said, 'Do you want me to bless the tree?'

I said, 'Not particularly. You could bless the sheep.'

He didn't think it was a good idea, and after a bit more sniffing around he revs up and revs off.

I wasn't very nice, I know, only he's a vicar.

He should be able to see that it's not a crime scene. It's a shrine.

I knelt down for a bit then sat on the seat.

They forecast rain so I put some bubble wrap down to cover the tracks.

★

I was late this morning and, when I got there, there's a bike parked in the layby and a woman standing there. I said, 'Is it you that leaves the flowers?' She said, 'Now and again. I've seen you many a time when I've been coming by and I've felt I ought to offer my condolences only . . . shy, I suppose.' She didn't look shy. Dyed hair, big bust, tattoos on her fingers. Leather from head to foot.

She said, 'You shouldn't kneel. He wasn't a saint.'

I said, 'I'll decide what he was.' She said, 'Can we sit down?' I said, 'You can. I'm all right.' So she sat on my seat.

She said, 'I didn't know Cliff well.'

I said, 'Is that what you called him?'

She said, 'What do you call him?'

I said, 'His name was Clifford.'

She said, 'Well, maybe that says it all. It was nothing to get worked up about. We just used to share a bacon sandwich.'

Well, I didn't say but I know for a fact he didn't like bacon. It didn't do for him.

'Strictly speaking,' she said, 'it was a bacon and egg sandwich. He had the egg. I had the bacon.'

I didn't ask what happened to the sandwiches I made him, wenged in a hedge somewhere, else fed to the ducks. They were lovely sandwiches.

'He gave his own sandwiches away', she said, 'to some of the young lads. Real gourmet sandwiches they were. They reckoned to fight over them. One of them said it was the one time in the week he tasted avocado.'

I sat down on the bench. 'Avocado, tomato and mozzarella they were. I'd make some for him and one for me. I'd think of us both eating them, me at home, him birdwatching. What lads?'

'He gave me one once,' she said, 'only I'm too much of a bacon fan. Birdwatching? Cliff? Really?'

She said, 'Don't misunderstand me but to tell you the truth you were a bit unexpected. We all thought he liked lads.'

I said, 'Clifford?'

'Oh, nothing happened, only he liked it when they took the piss. He was a lovely feller.'

'Well,' I said, 'he was shy.'

'Get him in his leathers,' she said, 'and he wasn't shy.'

I said, 'Was he racing?'

She said, 'Chasing more like.'

I said, 'Do they do that? What for?'

'Oh,' she said, 'just devilment. Get them on a bike and they do all sorts. Men.'

In the finish I came round to her a bit. I could see why Clifford liked her. And maybe she liked him. Because when she got back on her bike I could see she was crying.

I don't know what to think.

You don't cry over a bacon sandwich.

(*Pause.*)

Cliff.

★

84

In a story or a film, say, you'd cut to Lorna, who's turned over a new leaf and, got up in her dead husband's leathers, is now presiding over a transport café. And as bikers crowd the hatch and lather their sausages with ketchup, she dishes up the full English and you'd see it was the scene of the accident, only now transformed and a sign over the van, 'Cliff's Corner'.

And they'd come, because it's not just bacon, it's company. I say in a story or film but it was Betsy who suggested a caff, the blonde woman whom he palled on with. And we could have done it, the pair of us, out of the insurance money.

Only I didn't think so. Catering's no game and they travel in packs, bikers, half a dozen cooked breakfasts every five minutes, no fun on a Sunday morning, and even if it's just bacon and egg sandwiches it would soon choke you off.

Cliff would do it maybe. But not Clifford. He'd say, 'Don't go there, love.' And anyway I don't know Cliff.

I left it a while then I went up and cleared the site, dismantled my bench, sheep staring still. The tyre tracks were overgrown but I stamped them in anyway. Didn't kneel. Didn't even stand. So now it's back to being nowhere. But it was briefly a place because Clifford . . .

or Cliff . . . died there. And all along the roads of England for some people there are places now, spots where loved ones died. And, for some, even the emptiness of the mid-Atlantic will be a place, or the Indian Ocean. Happiness does it sometimes, but it's more often death that is the place-maker.

The police fetched round his helmet. Two of them, like they said. I've made them into hanging baskets. Got tomatoes in one, nasturtiums the other. That apart, there's nothing left much, except his computer . . . Cliff's, I suspect, rather than Clifford's. That'll be another bag of tricks, but which I can't open and shan't try.

Though I gather there are people who can do it.

Somebody came round doing a survey on bereavement, only I said mine wasn't typical, though it was a sort of mourning, going up there, keeping a vigil, finding out stuff.

I wish I'd known. (*She shakes her head.*) Or I wish I hadn't.

He was such a love.

# MURIEL

*Muriel* wasn't written for Covid but several years ago. It was the opening scene of a play that never got any further – with me a not infrequent occurrence. Had it proceeded to a conclusion, I think it might have ended with the situation reversed, Muriel seemingly dead with George rehearsing her obituary. A pity but still shorter is better – and you can't get much shorter than this.

Alan Bennett
May 2021

*Muriel* was originally recorded and released online
as part of Nottingham Playhouse's Spring Loaded season
in May 2021.


*Muriel*   Frances de la Tour
*Director*   Adam Penford

with thanks to Adrian Scarborough

*A woman, Muriel, sitting at a dressing table mirror cleaning her face as she talks, beginning to apply make-up.*

We're gathered here this afternoon, on Zoom, to remember George Hargreaves and to celebrate his life.

I know it's not the convention for a wife . . . or widow I should say . . . to speak at her husband's memorial but these are strange times . . . and George was never a conventional man, as many of you, I'm sure, can testify.

*(She fills up with tears but recovers.)*

Forgive me, I'm sorry . . .

In some ways it's wrong to speak of George as one person because there were several Georges. There was the George the public knew . . . bold, confident, successful, a power in the City.

There was the George I knew . . . the private George . . . measured . . . unhurried . . . George the gardener . . .

George prided himself on us never having spent a night apart in fifty-six years . . . And, of course, over this last unprecedented year, as with so many couples, he had been by my side day and night . . .

*A door bangs downstairs and she stops and listens.*

Is that you, George?

*George (out of view)* Who else? And I'm vaccinated.

*Muriel looks despairing.*